Experiential Exercises in Organization Theory and Design

Experiential Exercises in Organization Theory and Design

H. Eugene Baker III
University of North Florida

Steven K. Paulson
University of North Florida

THOMSON

SOUTH-WESTERN

Australia · Canada · Mexico · Singapore · Spain · United Kingdom · United States

THOMSON

SOUTH-WESTERN

Experiential Exercises in Organization Theory and Design, 1e

H. Eugene Baker III & Steven K. Paulson

Editor-in-Chief:
Jack Calhoun

Vice President/Team Director:
Michael P. Roche

Acquisitions Editor:
Joe Sabatino

Developmental Editor:
Emma F. Guttler

Sr. Production Editor:
Elizabeth A. Shipp

Sr. Marketing Manager:
Rob Bloom

Media Developmental Editor:
Kristen Meere

Media Production Editor:
Karen L. Schaffer

Manufacturing Coordinator:
Rhonda Utley

Production House:
Cover to Cover

Internal Designer:
B. Casey

Cover Designer:
B. Casey

Cover Images:
© PhotoDisc, Inc.

Printer:
Transcontinental Printing, Inc.
Louiseville, QC

For permission to use material from
this text or product, contact us by
Tel (800) 730-2214
Fax (800) 730-2215
http://www.thomsonrights.com

For more information
contact South-Western,
5191 Natorp Boulevard,
Mason, Ohio 45040.
Or you can visit our Internet site at:
http://www.swcollege.com

Dedications

To our families:
Shirley, Jeff, and Scott
Sally, Greg, Andy, and Eric

Table of Contents

Preface

The basic purpose of this book is to provide the student of business courses in organization theory with a set of classroom exercises that will help to illustrate and internalize the basic principles of the course. There is no other comparable book available, yet the experiential approach is widely used and considered to be very effective for this course material. The chapters of the book cover the most basic and widely covered topics of the field. Each chapter consists of a central focus, such as organizational power, production technology, or organizational culture, with all necessary materials to fully participate in three different exercises. The instructor's manual is a crucial document for the use of this book.

Taken together, the thirty exercises represent a wide variety in terms of time requirements: from less than five minutes to prepare to preparation requiring one hour or more; from very brief, ten minute "warm up's" to exercises that could take an entire 50 or 75 minute, or longer, class meeting period. The settings range from the students' own college to fast food chains to large corporate entities; some exercises are intended to be completed at the level of the individual, others in groups, and still others can been used either way. The exercises range from instrumentation-based, using assessment questionnaires, to actual creative production activities.

The exercises have all been tested in the authors' classes and are drawn from a variety of sources, including books created for other settings such as college classes on organizational behavior and organizational development and the management consulting profession. All of the exercises, which were created for related purposes, have been adapted specifically for the organization theory course.

In order to minimize the time necessary to become familiar with the exercises, they are presented in a uniform format. Once the instructor and students become familiar with the format, a minimal amount of time is necessary to assess the features of a given exercise. This format consists of three parts: (1) **objectives** of the exercise in terms of outcomes that can be expected to be attained by the class; (2) **process** in terms of the actual steps that the student should follow to successfully complete the exercise; and (3) **feedback**—a separate page that provides questions that allow for an individualized debriefing of the exercise for the student. In most cases, these items are presented with a range of requirements inasmuch as all of the exercises may be adjusted to conform to the specific objectives and teaching techniques used by the instructor.

The book is intended for junior, senior, and masters level courses in organization theory as traditionally taught in departments and colleges of business, education, and public administration. The exercises could also be adapted for use in courses in organizational behavior and organization development. In addition, the book is well suited for use in management training programs aimed at middle- and top-level managers.

Instructor's Resources

Instructor's Manual (0-324-16864-0). The Instructor's Manual to accompany this text contains practical information about each exercise to more effectively administer it in the classroom.

Website (http://baker.swcollege.com). The website includes additional information and instructor resources to facilitate use of this text.

Acknowledgments

In a very direct sense, we are grateful for the help our students have given over the past twelve years in providing feedback about various versions of the exercises that appear in this book. We could not have done the project without their help. Ms. Annette Driscoll provided outstanding manuscript preparation skill.

About the Authors

H. Eugene Baker III received his Ph.D. from the University of Florida. He is Professor of Management and Department Chair at the University of North Florida, College of Business Administration, Jacksonville, Florida. His specialties in both teaching and research include the organizational entry process, organizational socialization, organizational control mechanisms, organizational behavior, and organization theory. He has a special interest in teaching pedagogy and the use of experiential teaching techniques. Professor Baker has published several articles in both academic and professional publications.

Steven K. Paulson is Blanche and Luther Coggin Professor of Management at the University of North Florida, College of Business Administration, Jacksonville, Florida. His Ph.D. is from Iowa State University. His teaching interests include organizational theory, business ethics, and international business management. His research specialization is the area of interorganizational relationships with a focus on regional trade blocs. Dr. Paulson's publications appear in practitioner as well as academic journals.

Chapter 1

Exercise 1

I. Objective:

To become aware of, and familiar with, some of the topics that will be presented in the course.

II. Process:

Step 1. Introduction

Your instructor will select a key word for use in the association exercise.

Step 2. First Association

Develop as many words as possible that you "associate" with the key word. Remember, an "association" is the word or phrase that immediately comes to mind when a cue term is read or heard.

Step 3. Second Association

Your instructor will select a second word from the list generated by the class. Once again, identify as many "associations" as possible.

Step 4. Discussion

As a group, discuss the words generated during the exercise and how they relate to the course topics.

Exercise Feedback Form

Chapter 1   **Exercise #1**

Name: _____   **Student ID:** _____

1. Was your connotation of the "association word" positive or negative? Why?

2. Were the "association words" generated by the class what you anticipated?

3. How did the discussion of the "association exercise" clarify the direction of the course for you?

You may be asked to complete and turn in this form to your instructor.

Exercise 2

Exchange Game[2]

I. Objective:

To develop an understanding of various processes involved in organizational management.

II. Process:

Step 1. Introduction

The instructions are self-explanatory and are provided on "Exchange Card Number 1." We will play three rounds. Detach the playing card for Round 1 (p. 7).

Step 2. Scoring Round 1

Calculate scores for Round 1.

Step 3. Complete Round 2

Complete Round 2 according to instructions from your instructor.

Step 4. Score Round 2

Calculate score for Round 2.

Step 5. Complete Round 3

Complete Round 3 according to instructions from your instructor.

Step 6. Score Round 3

Calculate score for Round 3.

Step 7. Discussion

Discuss the various organizational techniques or practices that may have evolved as a result of the exercise.

Exchange Card Number 1

Object of the game:

To accumulate as many points as possible in a fixed time limit.

Scoring:

1 point for every different signature on either side of the card you hold when time is called.

Rules:

Your instructor will announce the beginning and ending of the playing time. You may only sign a card that you personally hold and control.

Exercise Feedback Form

Chapter 1   **Exercise #2**

Name: _____   **Student ID:** _____

1. Was the first round surprising? Why?

2. What ideas did you think of to increase your individual score?

3. How did the discussion of the exercise increase your awareness of the need to "organize"?

You may be asked to complete and turn in this form to your instructor.

Exercise 3

You'll Play the Role, So Why Not Pick the Part?

I. Objectives:

To help reinforce an understanding of the practical distinctions among five organizational "parts" and to learn about the stereotypical perceptions that people hold about others who are involved in different functional areas of the company.

II. Process:

Step 1. Introduction

Thoroughly familiarize yourself with the five organizational parts. See p. 17 for examples of the roles/functions found in each part.

Step 2. Your Preference

Rank the five organizational parts in *decreasing* order of your own *personal* preference for a major portion of your occupational career (i.e., #1 = highest preference, #5 = lowest preference) and, on the lines provided, write a one-sentence explanation for the ranking.

1. _____
   _____
   _____

2. _____
   _____
   _____

3. _____
   _____
   _____

4. _____
   _____
   _____

5. _____
   _____
   _____

Step 3. Group Formation

Based on your responses to the previous questions, or another criterion as directed by your instructor, you will be assigned to one of five types of groups. The groups may be equal in size, or they may be quite unequal in size. Regardless, each of the groups will correspond to one of the five organizational "parts." Your group will be located in an area of the classroom that is spatially separated from the others in a manner corresponding to p. 17. That is, the Top Management group should be located near the front of the classroom, the Technical Core in the back of the classroom, and the Middle Management group centered between the two; the Technical Support Staff and Administrative Support Staff should be located on the extreme right and left sides of the room respectively.

Step 4. Group Discussion

Although the exact assignment to the group will differ depending on the objectives of the course, the basic idea is to record (a) how you believe *you* would perceive *your* own organizational part and (b) as a member of this organizational part, how you believe you would perceive the other four organizational parts. Depending on your instructor's goals, these perceptions may focus on positive or negative attributes, cooperative or conflicting processes, or other issues.

Step 5. Group Report

Select one of your group members to report the conclusion of your discussion. A very brief statement (1–5 words) should suffice for each one of the five perceptions. Note: past *experience* suggests that there may be derisive reactions to your statements (especially between staff and line units and between the Top Management group and *all* other units), but *theory* suggests that all functions are necessary so pay little attention to detractors!

Step 6. Class Discussion

Depending upon the objectives of the course, this exercise will point out different principles. Nevertheless, on the basis of your experience in this exercise, how difficult do you believe it would be for people in different functional areas of a company to form inaccurate stereotypes of one another? How can these stereotypes by avoided? What other theories are relevant in this situation? Does TQM (Total Quality Management), for example, relate to these issues? Is organizational culture an important consideration?

Perceptions Scorecard

Your Part: _____

Perceptions held by your part about:

Top Management: _____

_____

_____

_____

_____

_____

Middle
Management: _____

_____

_____

_____

_____

_____

Technical Core: _____

_____

_____

_____

_____

_____

Technical
Support Staff: _____

_____

_____

_____

_____

_____

Administrative
Support Staff: _____

_____

_____

_____

_____

_____

Exercise Feedback Form

Chapter 1   **Exercise #3**

Name: _____   **Student ID:** _____

1. How accurate do you believe your perceptions of each "part" of the organization were? Why?

2. How accurate do you believe the perceptions of others of your part were? Why?

3. How might you reconcile the differences in perception?

You may be asked to complete and turn in this form to your instructor.

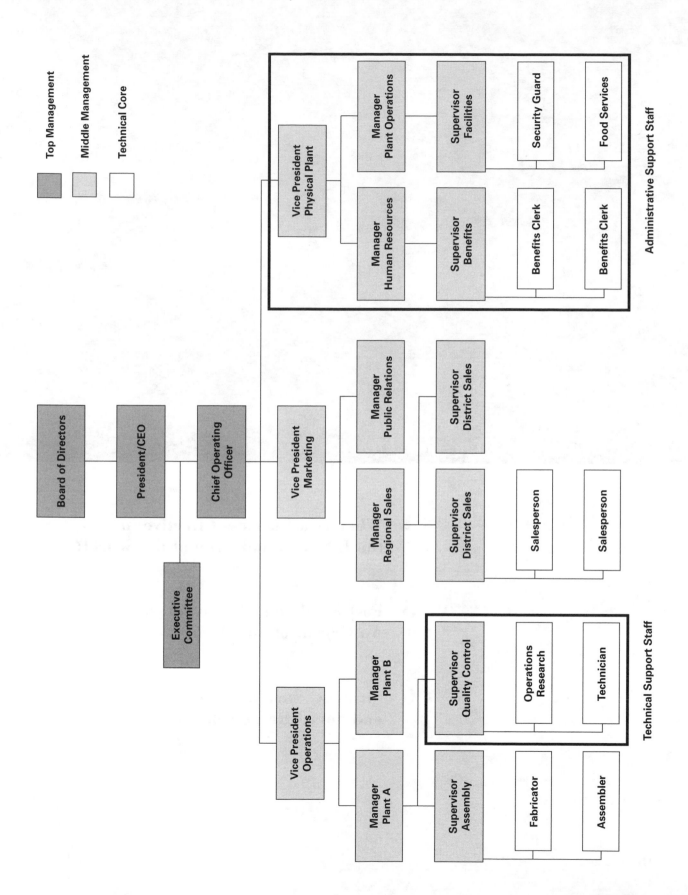

Chapter 2

Strategy, Design, and Effectiveness

Exercise 4

When Is a Business Effective in the U.S. . . . and Around the World?[3]

I. Objectives:

To learn about an eight-level hierarchy of purposes that U.S. corporate executives hold for business enterprises and to compare such rankings with those of several different nations.

II. Process:

Step 1. Rank Order of Goals of Business Executives

In a series of cross-cultural studies, George W. England asked business executives to assess the relative importance of eight goals that are often mentioned as basic to business activity. Based on your general knowledge and intuition, place the numbers 1 through 8 in each column of "Form A" to indicate your opinion of the relative importance of the goals in the countries indicated; let 1 = most important and 8 = least important. Although some goals may seem more similar than others, for the purpose of this exercise use only whole numbers and each number only once to indicate the rank order.

Step 2. Time Relevance and/or Group Consensus

Based on the objectives for the course, your instructor may ask you to fill in "Form B" with somewhat different instructions than those of Step 1.

Form A | *Business Goals in Five Countries*

Business goals	Australia	India	Japan	Korea	U.S.
High productivity					
Industry leadership					
Employee welfare					
Organizational stability					
Profit maximization					
Organizational efficiency					
Social welfare					
Organizational growth					

Form B | *Business Goals in Five Countries*

Business goals	Australia	India	Japan	Korea	U.S.
High productivity					
Industry leadership					
Employee welfare					
Organizational stability					
Profit maximization					
Organizational efficiency					
Social welfare					
Organizational growth					

Exercise Feedback Form

Chapter 2   **Exercise #4**

Name: _____   **Student ID:** _____

1. What surprised you most about the actual rankings of business executives? Why?

2. Why do you imagine that "Profit" was not consistently ranked number 1 in spite of the almost universal definition of business as a "profit seeking organization"?

3. What items do you believe should be added to the list of characteristics?

You may be asked to complete and turn in this form to your instructor.

Exercise 5

Fast Food and Effectiveness: An Organizational Diagnosis[4]

I. Objectives:

To diagnose an organization in terms of goals, policies, procedures, structure, climate, technology, environment, job design, communication, and leadership, and to compare and contrast two organizations on these variables.

II. Process:

Step 1. Introduction

A critical first step in improving or changing any organization is *diagnosing*, or analyzing, its present functioning. Many change and organization development efforts fall short of their objectives because this important step was not taken, or was conducted superficially. To illustrate this, imagine how you would feel if you went to your doctor complaining of stomach pains, and the doctor recommended surgery without conducting any tests, without obtaining any further information, and without a careful physical examination. You would probably switch doctors! Yet, managers often attempt major changes with correspondingly little diagnostic work in advance. In this exercise, you will be asked to conduct a group diagnosis of two different organizations in the fast food business. The exercise will provide an opportunity to integrate much of the knowledge you have gained in other exercises and in studying other topics. Your task will be to describe the organizations as carefully as you can in terms of several key organizational concepts. Although the organizations are probably very familiar to you, try to step back and look at them as though you were seeing them for the first time.

Step 2. Your Assignment

The group will be formed into subgroups. Your assignment is described as follows:

One experience most people in this country have shared is that of dining in the hamburger establishment known as McDonald's. In fact, someone has claimed that 25th-century archaeologists may dig into the ruins of our present civilization and conclude that 20th-century religion was devoted to the worship of golden arches.

Your group, Fastalk Consultants, is known as the shrewdest but most insightful management consulting firm in the country. You have been hired by Mr. Bhik Maak, McDonald's president, to make recommendations for improving the motivation and performance of personnel in their franchise operations. Let us assume that key job activities in franchise operations are food preparation, order-taking and dealing with customers, and routine clean-up operations.

Recently Mr. Maak has come to suspect that his company's competitors such as Burger King, Wendy's, Jack in the Box, various pizza establishments, and others are making heavy inroads into McDonald's market. He has also hired a market research firm to investigate and compare the relative merits of the sandwiches, french fries, and drinks served in McDonald's and the competitor, and has asked the market research firm to assess the advertising campaigns of the two organizations. Hence, you will not need to be concerned with marketing issues, except as they may have an impact on employee behavior. The president wants *you* to look into the *organization* of the franchises to determine the strengths and weaknesses of each. Select a competitor that gives McDonald's a good "run for its money" in your area.

Mr. Maak has established an unusual contract with you. ***He wants you to make your recommendations based upon your observations as a customer.*** He does not want you to do a complete diagnosis with interviews, surveys, or behind-the-scenes observations. He wants your report in two parts.

A. Given his organization's goals of profitability, sales volume, fast and courteous service, and cleanliness, he wants an analysis that will *compare and contrast McDonald's and the competitor* in terms of the following concepts:

Organizational goals
Organizational structure
Technology
Environment
Employee motivation
Communication
Leadership style
Policies/procedures/rules/standards
Job design
Organizational climate

B. Given the corporate goals listed under point A, what specific actions might McDonald's management and franchise owners take in the following areas to achieve these goals (profitability, sales volume, fast and courteous service, and cleanliness)?

Job design and workflow
Organization structure (at the individual restaurant level)
Employee incentives
Leadership
Employee selection

Step 3. Initial Assessment

How do McDonald's and the competitor differ in these aspects? Which company has the best approach?

Step 4. Some Guidelines

A. Substantiate your recommendations by reference to one or more theories of motivation, leadership, small groups, or job design.
B. The president wants concrete, specific, and practical recommendations. Avoid vague generalizations such as "improve communications" or "increase trust." Say very clearly *how* management can improve organizational performance.
C. As you make your group presentation, the rest of the class will play the role of the top management executive committee. They may be a bit skeptical. They will ask tough questions. They will have to be sold on your ideas.
D. You will have *10 minutes* in which to present your ideas to the executive committee and to respond to their questions.

Step 5. Outside of Class Preparation

Complete the assignment by going as a group to one McDonald's and one competitor's restaurant. If possible, have a meal in each place. To get a more valid comparison, visit a McDonald's and a competitor located in the same area. After observing each restaurant, meet with your group and prepare your 10-minute report to the executive committee.

Step 6. Class Report

In class, each subgroup will present its report to the rest of the group, who will act as the executive committee. The group leader will appoint a timekeeper to be sure that each subgroup sticks to its 10-minute time limit.

Exercise Feedback Form

Chapter 2   **Exercise #5**

Name: _____   **Student ID:** _____

1. Look, again, at the items of the "A" list in Step 2 of the process section of the exercise. Which one of these items was the most difficult to document? Why? Which one was the easiest to document? Why?

2. After participating in this exercise, will your perceptions of fast food restaurants be somewhat different? Why or why not?

3. How do you believe that other retail stores would compare to those in the fast food industry? Would there be very large differences? Why or why not?

You may be asked to complete and turn in this form to your instructor.

Exercise 6

Strategy, Stakeholders, and Social Responsibility[5]

I. Objectives:

To become familiar with the four strategic positions described by Miles and Snow, to experience zero-sum decision making as individuals or as members of groups, to develop an awareness of various stakeholder groups that are relevant to financial decisions of manufacturing organizations in the community, and to experience the complexity of making operational and financial decisions with an awareness of the social responsibility of the firm.

II. Process:

Step 1. Exercise Scenario

You are the plant manager (or a member of the Plant Management Group) for a small manufacturing plant that has developed (i.e., the instructor has assigned) one particular strategic approach (defender, prospector, reactor, or analyzer). You have the authority to allocate funds, as you deem appropriate. However, you also must be able to justify your decisions to top management, your employees, the community, and other interested people from the perspective of the strategic approach that has been developed (assigned). Although the plant has been operating at an acceptable level, there is always the need to improve operations. You have argued that with extra funding, you could make significant improvements in the plant's operations. The company has given you the opportunity to prove the merit of your ideas by allocating an extra $1 million to your budget. There are a series of constraints, as follows:

1. You must spend the money for the projects listed in Step 2.
2. You must spend, for each project, at least the amount listed under the first column (from the left) and you may spend only the amounts listed.
3. You may have to justify your allocation decisions to a committee of managers, employees, and other members of the business community. These decisions *must* be consistent with the strategic approach you have been assigned.
4. Any money you do not spend must be returned to the parent company and is lost to you.

Step 2. Permissible Project Allocation Categories

Projects	Alternative A	Alternative B	Alternative C
Market research	Maintain current market share Cost $50,000	Study penetration of national market Cost $200,000	Explore options for international business Cost $300,000
Dividends	Pay none Cost $0	Pay $.50 per share Cost $150,000	Pay $1 per share and attract investors Cost $300,000
Wage increases	Maintain current levels Cost $0	5% cost of living increase Cost $150,000	Cost of living and 5% merit Cost $300,000
Pollution control	Kill everything within 1 mile Cost $0	Comply with new legislation Cost $150,000	Significantly reduce pollution Cost $250,000
Discrimination	Hire qualified white males and risk a discrimination suit Cost $140,000	Hire a few minorities and hope for the best Cost $250,000	Hire "hard core" unemployed and train and generate much goodwill Cost $350,000
Research and development	Leave well enough alone Cost $0	Research means of reducing manufacturing costs Cost $150,000	Seek ways to increase brand loyalty Cost $250,000
Enhance public image	Host wine and cheese party for local officials Cost $10,000	Hold weekend retreat for major stockholders Cost $150,000	Rent resort for a week to gain support of major financial institutions Cost $250,000
Compensation	Money is unimportant Pay self $0	Pay self $50,000 in salary and fringe benefits	Pay self $100,000

Step 3. Make Decisions Concerning Financial Allocations

Market research: $ _____
Dividends: $ _____
Wage increases: $ _____
Pollution control: $ _____
Discrimination: $ _____
Research and development: $ _____
Enhance public image: $ _____
Compensation: $ _____
　Total: $ _____

Exercise Feedback Form

Chapter 2   **Exercise #6**

Name: _____   **Student ID:** _____

1. Even though this exercise was fictitious, did certain decisions make you feel personally uncomfortable? Why or why not?

2. How much influence did financial allocation restrictions, such as the need to budget exactly $1,000,000, have on your decisions?

3. If you could select any one of the four strategic orientations to follow in your business career, which one would it be? Why?

You may be asked to complete and turn in this form to your instructor.

Chapter 3

Organization Structure

Exercise 7

The Apple-Orange Company Structure[6]

I. Objective:

To stimulate thinking about the fact that there are several different ways to organize work.

II. Process:

Step 1. Introduction

Read the description of the Apple-Orange Company. When you have finished, answer the questions that follow.

THE APPLE-ORANGE COMPANY

The Apple-Orange Company grows and markets apples and oranges in the southeastern United States. Apple-Orange has been in the produce business for the past 50 years and has some of the finest land for growing these fruits. They have also been quite successful in marketing their product. Up until now, Apple-Orange has been a family business run by old John Graves, whose father and uncle started the business. His son Carl has been working as his assistant since Carl returned from Vietnam.

Basically there are three major sets of activities that must be accomplished to grow and market Apple-Orange's products. One group of workers and managers works in the fields, handling the growing and harvesting of the apples and oranges.

Another group of workers and managers works in development research. This group is comprised largely of agricultural scientists who attempt to improve the varieties grown and to increase crop yield.

Marketing is handled by several sales personnel who call on wholesalers and fruit distributors in the region. The sales staff is very large and has been, like all other employees, very effective.

John and Carl have been managing Apple-Orange without many formal policies and procedures. The company has few set rules, procedures, and job descriptions. John believes that once people know their job, they should and would do it well.

However, Apple-Orange has grown fairly large, and John and Carl both believe that it is now necessary to develop a more formal organization structure. They have invited D. J. Blair, a noted management consultant, to help them. D. J. has told them that they have, basically, two choices. One is a functional organization structure, and the second is a product-based organization structure. These two different forms are shown in the figure on page 36.

Step 2. Discussion Questions

Based on your own knowledge, guesses, and common sense, do you believe it is possible to "mix apples and oranges" in this case? That is, would your choice of structure be functional or product? Why do you prefer this structure for the case?

The Apple-Orange Company

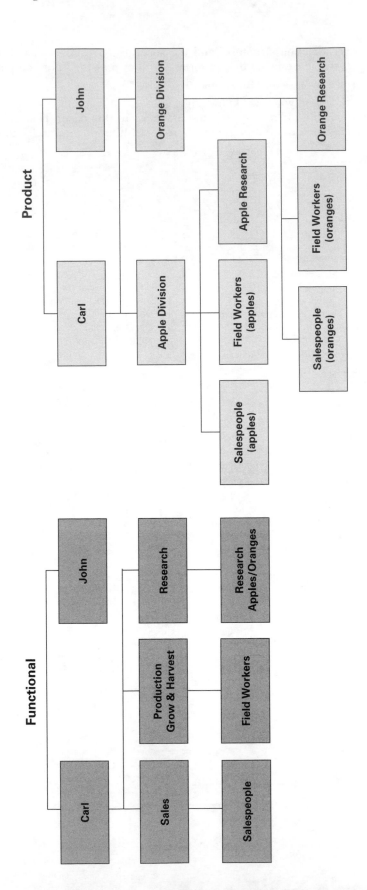

Exercise Feedback Form

Chapter 3   Exercise #7

Name: _____   Student ID: _____

1. What are some of the advantages of retaining the current structure of the company?

2. What are some of the advantages of implementing a functional structure? The disadvantages?

3. What are some of the advantages of implementing a product structure? The disadvantages?

You may be asked to complete and turn in this form to your instructor.

Exercise 8

Words-In-Sentences, Inc. [7]

I. Objectives:

To experiment with designing and operating an organization and to compare production and quality outputs under different organization structures and/or leadership styles.

II. Process:

Step 1. Introduction

In this exercise, you will form a "mini-organization" with several other people. You will also compete with other companies in your industry. The success of your company will depend on your (1) objectives, (2) planning, (3) organization structure, and (4) quality control. It may also depend on leadership style. It is important, therefore, that you spend some time thinking about the best design for your organization.

Step 2. Group Formation

Form companies and assign work places. The total group should be subdivided into small groups of comparable size. Since the success of any one group will not be dependent on size alone, do not be concerned if some groups are larger than others. *Each group should consider itself a company.* Your instructor may designate a manager and give him/her special directions.

Step 3. Detailed Instructions

Read the following "Directions" and ask the group leader about any points that need clarification. Everyone should be familiar with the task before beginning Step 4.

FIRM AND INDUSTRY SETTING

You are a small company that manufactures words and then packages them in meaningful (English language) sentences. Market research has established that sentences of at least three words but not more than six words each are in demand. Therefore, packaging, distribution, and sales should be set up for three-to-six-word sentences.

The "words-in-sentences" (WIS) industry is highly competitive; several new firms have recently entered what appears to be an expanding market. Since raw materials, technology, and pricing are all standard for the industry, your ability to compete depends on two factors: (1) volume and (2) quality.

GROUP TASK

Your group must design and participate in running a WIS company. You should design your organization to be as efficient as possible during each production run. After the first production run, you will have an opportunity to reorganize your company if you want to.

RAW MATERIALS

For each production run, you will be given a "raw material word or phrase." The letters found in the word or phrase serve as the raw materials available to produce new words in sentences. For example, if the raw material word is "organization," you could produce the following words and sentence: "Nat ran to a zoo."

PRODUCTION STANDARDS

There are several rules that have to be followed in producing "words-in-sentences." If these rules are not followed, your output will not meet production specifications and will not pass quality control inspection.

1. The same letter may appear only as often in a manufactured word as it appears in the raw material word or phrase; for example, "organization" has two *o*'s. Thus "zoo" is legitimate, but zoology is not. It has too many *o*'s.
2. Raw material letters can be used again in different manufactured words.
3. A manufactured word may be used only once in a sentence and in only one sentence during a production run; if a word—for example, *a*—is used once in a sentence, it is out of stock.
4. A new word may not be made by adding *s* to form the plural of an already used manufactured word.
5. A word is defined by its spelling, not its meaning.
6. Nonsense words or nonsense sentences are unacceptable.
7. All words must be in the English language.
8. Names and places are acceptable.
9. Slang is not acceptable.

MEASURING PERFORMANCE

The output of your WIS company is measured by the ***total number of acceptable words*** that are packaged in sentences. The sentences must be legible, listed on no more than two sheets of paper, and handed to the Quality Control Review Board at the completion of each production run.

DELIVERY

Delivery must be made to the Quality Control Review Board 30 seconds after the end of each production run.

QUALITY CONTROL

If any word in a sentence does not meet the standards previously set forth, ***all*** the words in the sentence will be rejected. The Quality Control Review Board (composed of one member from each company) is the final arbiter of acceptability. In the event of a tie vote on the Review Board, a coin toss will determine the outcome.

Step 4. Organization Design Phase

Design your organization using as many group members as you see fit to produce your "words-in-sentences." There are many potential ways of organizing. Since some are more efficient than others, you may want to consider the following:

1. What is your company's objective?
2. How will you achieve your objective? How should you plan your work, given the time allowed?
3. What division of labor, authority, and responsibility is most appropriate, given your objective, your task, and the technology?

4. Which group members are most qualified to perform certain tasks?
5. Assign one member of your group to serve on the Quality Review Board. This person may also participate in production runs.

Step 5. Production Run 1

1. The group leader will hand each WIS company a sheet with a raw material word or phrase.
2. When the instructor announces "Begin production," you are to manufacture as many words as possible and package them in sentences for delivery to the Quality Control Review Board.
3. When the group leader announces "Stop production," you will have 30 seconds to deliver your output to the Quality Control Review Board. Output received after 30 seconds does not meet the delivery schedule and will not be counted.

Step 6. Production Review Control Run 1

1. The designated members from the companies of the Quality Control Review Board review output from each company. The total output should be recorded (after quality control approval) on the board or easel.
2. While the Board is completing its task, each WIS company should discuss what happened during Production Run 1.

Step 7. Organizational Planning for Run 2

Each company should evaluate its performance and organization. Companies may reorganize for Run 2.

Step 8. Production Run 2

1. The group leader will hand each WIS company a sheet with a raw material word or phrase.
2. Proceed as in Step 5 (Production Run 1).

Step 9. Production Review Control Run 2

1. The Quality Control Review Board will review each company's output and record it on the board or easel. The total for Runs 1 and 2 should be tallied.
2. While the Board is completing its task, each WIS company should prepare an organization chart depicting its structure for both production runs. If the group had a "manager," what effect did the manager's leadership style have on the group's motivation and production?

Step 10. Class Discussion

Discuss this exercise as a total group. The group leader will provide discussion questions. Each company should share the organization charts it prepared in Step 9.

Exercise Feedback Form

Chapter 3   **Exercise #8**

Name: _____   **Student ID:** _____

1. How would you classify the technology of your WIS company?

2. What theory would predict the most appropriate structure for the company?

3. How did leadership style affect the group?

You may be asked to complete and turn in this form to your instructor.

Exercise 9

The Club Ed Exercise[8]

I. Objective:

To explore structural alternatives and organizational systems options that are available to aid in the design and redesign of a changing organization.

II. Process:

Step 1. Introduction

Read the following scenario:

Determined never to shovel snow again, you are establishing a new resort business on a small Caribbean island. The building of the resort is under way and it is scheduled to open a year from now. You decide it is time to draw up an organizational chart for this new venture, Club Ed. What jobs do you need to have covered? What tasks need to be done? What services will you provide? Work in small groups to draw your organization chart and be prepared to present your design and to answer the following questions: What should it include? and Why should it look like this?

Step 2. Presentation of Design

Your instructor will select one or two groups to present their designs and lead the class discussion.

Step 3. Subsequent Designs

Your instructor will provide you with additional information that must be integrated into your decision and design process. You will be provided with time to develop a response.

Step 4. Class Discussion

One or two groups will be selected to present their response.

Exercise Feedback Form

Chapter 3   **Exercise #9**

Name: _____   **Student ID:** _____

1. How does the nature of an organization's technology influence organization design?

2. How can we measure the effectiveness of Club Ed? How does feedback about effectiveness influence organization design?

3. How can Club Ed structure itself as an adaptive organization? Does it always have to react to environmental changes or are there some ways it can be proactive?

You may be asked to complete and turn in this form to your instructor.

Chapter 4

Environment

Exercise 10

Organizational Diagnosis of the College Setting[9]

I. Objective:

To use organizational theory as a basis for diagnosing and making recommendations concerning the fit between the environment of a college and the internal structure of that college.

II. Process:

Step 1. Complete Questionnaire

When assigned by the instructor, answer the questions of Parts I, II, and III.

Part I — *Environmental Uncertainty (EU)*

	To little or no extent	To a slight extent	To a moderate extent	To a considerable extent	To a very great extent
To what extent . . .					
• does the government frequently develop requirements, regulations, and policies that directly affect your organization?	❑	❑	❑	❑	❑
• do frequent technological changes or advances make current products or operations obsolete, requiring major changes?	❑	❑	❑	❑	❑
• is there intense competition among organizations in your field?	❑	❑	❑	❑	❑
• do different clients of your organization require individualized attention?	❑	❑	❑	❑	❑
• does the environment in which your organization operates change unpredictably?	❑	❑	❑	❑	❑
Add the checks in each column:					
Multiply as indicated:	× 1	× 2	× 3	× 4	× 5
Add: EU = _____ =	+	+	+	+	+

Part II   *Structural Complexity (SC)*

	To little or no extent	To a slight extent	To a moderate extent	To a considerable extent	To a very great extent
To what extent . . .					
• do different groups or units operate on very different time lines (e.g., long-range versus short-term)?	❏	❏	❏	❏	❏
• do different groups or units in this organization have quite different task goals (as opposed to many groups doing the same or similar things)?	❏	❏	❏	❏	❏
• do groups or units in this organization differ in terms of their emphasis or concern for people versus concern for getting the job done?	❏	❏	❏	❏	❏
• do groups or units differ in how formal things are (e.g., emphasis on adherence to rules, regulations, and policies, following the chain of command, etc., vs. few formal rules, much informal contact, etc.)?	❏	❏	❏	❏	❏
• are there many different specialized units, groups, or departments in this organization?	❏	❏	❏	❏	❏
Add the checks in each column:					
Multiply as indicated:	× 1	× 2	× 3	× 4	× 5
Add: SC = _____ =	+	+	+	+	+

Part III   *Structural Formalization (SF)*

	To little or no extent	To a slight extent	To a moderate extent	To a considerable extent	To a very great extent
To what extent . . .					
• are rules and policies an important basis for inter-unit coordination?	❑	❑	❑	❑	❑
• are formal plans a major basis for inter-unit coordination?	❑	❑	❑	❑	❑
• are formal liaisons (individuals or teams) a significant basis for inter-unit coordination?	❑	❑	❑	❑	❑
• are regular meetings and problem-solving sessions for mutual adjustment an important basis for inter-unit coordination?	❑	❑	❑	❑	❑
• is there a great deal of formal effort devoted to inter-unit coordination?	❑	❑	❑	❑	❑
Add the checks in each column:					
Multiply as indicated:	× 1	× 2	× 3	× 4	× 5
Add: SF = _____ =	+	+	+	+	+

Step 2. Compute Summary Score

PART I: Environmental Uncertainty (EU) = _____

PART II: Structural Complexity   (SC) = _____

PART III: Structural Formalization   (SF) = _____

Scores range from 5 to 25 on each scale:

HIGH   = 20–25

MODERATE = 11–19

LOW   = 5–10

Exercise Feedback Form

Chapter 4   **Exercise #10**

Name: _____   **Student ID:** _____

1. How many class members have organizations with EU-SC-SF "fit"?

2. What were the most common types of "mis-fit"? Why?

3. How would you go about reducing the SC score? Is it easier to change the SC score than it is to change the SF score? Why or why not?

You may be asked to complete and turn in this form to your instructor.

Exercise 11

I. Objectives:

To understand that there are many factors outside the organization that have a great impact on decisions made inside the organization, to realize that most of these factors evolve as the result of interaction between groups with differing views, and to develop the ability to consider the views of several external factors or "stakeholders" while maintaining a primary focus of the organization itself.

II. Process:

Step 1. Exercise Familiarization

After your instructor has assigned a case issue and a position to take (A, B, or sometimes C), read the provided issue case scenario carefully.

Step 2. General Strategy

Work in groups or individually, as the instructor assigns, and decide upon a general philosophical approach to presenting your position on the issue.

Step 3. Specific Arguments

Develop a series of specific arguments based on the general strategy developed in Step 2 and record these according to the instructions of the instructor.

ISSUE CASE SCENARIOS

Issue Case 1

Due to a number of recent injuries and deaths of children a number of consumer groups have demanded that toy companies recall a number of products and institute a new safety testing program for all of these products. The toy companies respond that they do have a large testing and safety program now. They further state that all of their products are clearly labeled with the age group that is appropriate for the toy, safety instructions, and a toll-free telephone number that consumers can call with problems and suggestions. They note that the majority of injuries have occurred when the instructions were not followed or the toys were given to children younger than the age noted on the package.

    A. Consumer Group View
    B. Toy Industry View

Issue Case 2

During contract negotiations, the union insists that now that the company is in good financial condition the employees must have a large wage increase to close the gap created by previously limiting increases to allow the company to recover its financial health. The company states that, although its condition has improved, if this large wage increase is approved, it will no longer be able to be competitive in its pricing and will again face financial hardship.

    A. Union View
    B. Company View

Issue Case 3

One governmental regulatory agency is supporting legislation that will require additional safety restraints in automobiles while another agency is demanding increased mileage and reduced air pollution. The automobile manufacturers argue that these additional regulations, in addition to those already in effect, will have a disastrous effect on the industry by increasing the initial cost of automobiles and their maintenance costs. In addition to increasing unemployment resulting from reduced sales, such regulations will reduce the number of families who will be able to afford a car.

    A. Government View
    B. Automobile Industry View

Issue Case 4

A large insurance company is under fire by several groups who have noted that although the company's work force is 70% female that none of the senior management positions are held by women. The groups state that if some action is not taken to rectify this problem they will start a nationwide boycott of the company. In the past this type of boycott has worked very well for the groups. The company maintains that it has made every effort to find women for senior management positions but has not been able to. The vast majority of women employed by the firm are in clerical positions. Although they have several educational programs to encourage their employees to become prepared for management positions, these programs are only a few years old and it will be several years before those participating in the programs will be ready to move into senior management.

    A. Women's Group View
    B. Insurance Company View

Issue Case 5

Local environmental agencies have filed notice with the local steel mill that it can no longer dump its waste into the river that serves as the town's source of drinking water. Some of the pollutants have been linked with increased cancer in the area. The mill's managers argue that this requirement to find a new method of waste disposal would increase the operating costs so much that, given the strong foreign competition, they would have to close the mill. The local people say that the mill is the major employer in town and if the mill is closed over half the population will be unemployed. They would rather have jobs and bad water than no jobs.

    A. Environmental Agency View
    B. Steel Mill View
    C. Employee View

Issue Case 6

Several airlines serving the same regional area have suggested that they agree on fares for certain routes. If they continue the current fare war they will not be able to continue service to several areas since only certain routes are profitable enough to continue under such low fare levels. The people in the towns that may no longer have service strongly support this idea. The government agencies involved are clear that such an agreement on price is illegal; if the airlines attempt to fix fares, they will be fined.

    A. Airline View
    B. Government View
    C. Local Town View

Step 4. Position Summary

Issue Case #1.

Circle one: Position A   B

Discuss the General Strategy and Specific Arguments you or your group developed.

Issue Case #2.

Circle one: Position A   B

Discuss the General Strategy and Specific Arguments you or your group developed.

Issue Case #3.

Circle one: Position A   B

Discuss the General Strategy and Specific Arguments you or your group developed.

Issue Case #4.

Circle one: Position A   B

Discuss the General Strategy and Specific Arguments you or your group developed.

Issue Case #5.

Circle one: Position A   B   C

Discuss the General Strategy and Specific Arguments you or your group developed.

Issue Case #6.

Circle one: Position A   B   C

Discuss the General Strategy and Specific Arguments you or your group developed.

Exercise Feedback Form

Chapter 4   Exercise #11

Name: _____   Student ID: _____

1. What difficulties did you experience when you were developing views for stakeholder groups?

2. Many types of stakeholders are illustrated in this exercise. Describe two additional types of stakeholders that business managers might have to take into account that are not illustrated by the exercise.

3. Identify any one of the issue cases that you were assigned in the exercise and the stakeholder view with which you personally would feel most comfortable. Why would you feel most comfortable with this view?

You may be asked to complete and turn in this form to your instructor.

Exercise 12

I. Objective:

To explore the relative merits of three different approaches to developing cooperative relationships among competing businesses in order to successfully compete against a common external threat to their individual markets.

II. Process:

Step 1. The Scenario

The instructor will assign you to one of the three grocery stores that are described in the following "Small Town Scenario." Read the entire "Small Town Scenario" concerning the situation facing your grocery store and two other grocery stores in a small town.

SMALL TOWN SCENARIO

You live and work in a small town with three very competitive, small, locally owned grocery stores facing survival-threatening competition from a large supermarket chain that plans to build a super-supermarket in the center of town. You are part of the ownership group of one of these grocery stores; your group has decided to establish an interorganizational relationship with one or both of the other stores as a means of reducing uncertainty, yet your organization wants to retain as much of the decision-making autonomy as possible. You hire a consultant who has calculated the relative "payoffs" of alternative courses of Interorganizational Relations (IOR) actions. Soon, a member of your group will meet with representatives of both of the other stores and then privately with the representative of each of the stores; thus three negotiations in which you will agree to some form of IOR. The three stores are as follows: <u>A</u>mericana Grocery Store specializes in fresh produce but also sells meat and grocery items; <u>B</u>uddy's Grocery Store specializes in locally butchered meat but also sells produce and grocery items; <u>C</u>orner Grocery Store specializes in gourmet and ethnic specialty grocery items but also sells produce and meat. Note that "specializes" means a long tradition of low prices, high quality, and much variety because of personal relationships outside of the organization and technical knowledge of the owners.

Step 2. The Payoff

Familiarize yourself with the following IOR Payoff Schedule.

A. If your store is not included in any mutual IOR → 0 points

B. If your store is included in a mutual dyadic IOR:

    contract   → 15 points
    cooptation → 12 points
    coalition   → 9 points

C. If your store is included in a mutual triad IOR:

    contract   → 10 points
    cooptation → 8 points
    coalition   → 6 points

Step 3. The Decision

When the instructor asks you for your grocery store's decision, write the following sentence on a piece of paper and fill in the blanks without consulting any other store. "Our store, the _____, hereby agrees to enter into a _____ type of interorganizational relationship with _____ for the purpose of decreasing competitive uncertainty while maintaining a degree of autonomy."

Exercise Feedback Form

Chapter 4   **Exercise #12**

Name: _____   **Student ID:** _____

1. How could the rules of the exercise be modified to allow for more trust among the three stores? Would this have made the IOR negotiation easier?

2. If the rules of the exercise had allowed for more complex forms of IOR to be designed, what might one of those have been?

3. Are you aware of a real situation that is similar to the small town scenario of this exercise? How did that situation work out? What form(s) of IOR were involved?

You may be asked to complete and turn in this form to your instructor.

Chapter 5

Exercise 13

Measuring Technology[11]

I. Objective:

To assess the extent of task variability and problem analyzability present in various organizational units.

II. Process:

Task variability and problem analyzability can be measured in an organizational unit by answering the following ten questions. Scores are derived from responses scored on a one-to-seven scale for each question.

Step 1. Complete Questionnaire

Complete the questionnaire for each of the following departments. Use the symbol for each department, i.e., Computer Operations—A, Methodology Department—B, etc.

- **A.** Computer Operations (i.e., mounting tapes, data batch processing, printer setup)
- **B.** Methodology Department (i.e., survey development, survey specifications, workflow process analysis)
- **C.** Human Resources Training Group (i.e., rewrite training materials, update training manuals)
- **D.** Computer Systems Analysis (i.e., customizing user computer systems, developing new systems applications)

Step 2. Scoring

Transfer your score for each item on the questionnaire to the scoring table. Calculate the average for each of the variables as indicated.

Step 3. Discussion

Meet in small groups to discuss and compare individual responses for each department.

QUESTIONNAIRE

The following questions pertain to the normal, usual, day-to-day pattern of work carried out by yourself and the people in your work unit. Please check the appropriate answers.

1. How many tasks are the same from day to day?

Very few of them			Some of them		Most of them	
1	2	3	4	5	6	7

2. To what extent is there a clearly known way to do the major types of work you normally encounter?

To a small extent			To some extent		To a great extent	
1	2	3	4	5	6	7

3. To what extent would you say your work is routine?

To a small extent			To some extent		To a great extent	
1	2	3	4	5	6	7

4. To what extent is there a clearly defined body of knowledge of subject matter that can guide you in doing your work?

To a small extent			To some extent		To a great extent	
1	2	3	4	5	6	7

5. To what extent is there an understandable sequence of steps that can be followed in doing your work?

To a small extent			To some extent		To a great extent	
1	2	3	4	5	6	7

6. People in this unit do about the same job in the same way most of the time.

To a small extent			To some extent		To a great extent	
1	2	3	4	5	6	7

7. Basically, unit members perform repetitive activities in doing their jobs.

To a small extent			To some extent		To a great extent	
1	2	3	4	5	6	7

8. To do your work, to what extent can you actually rely on established procedures and practices?

To a small extent   To some extent   To a great extent

1   2   3   4   5   6   7

9. How repetitious are your duties?

Very little   Moderate amount   Very much

1   2   3   4   5   6   7

10. To what extent is there an understandable sequence of steps that can be followed in carrying out your work?

To a small extent   To some extent   To a great extent

1   2   3   4   5   6   7

SCORING TABLE

Task Variability	Problem Analyzability
Item 1:	Item 2:
Item 3:	Item 4:
Item 6:	Item 5:
Item 7:	Item 8:
Item 9:	Item 10:
Total	Total
Divide by 5	Divide by 5
Average score:	Average score:

Exercise Feedback Form

Chapter 5   **Exercise #13**

Name: _____   **Student ID:** _____

1. What similarities/differences exist among the four departments in the exercise?

2. What special issues arise as a result of the level of analyzability and variability present in a department? How might the structure be impacted?

3. What levels of analyzability and variability did you find for your department? Do the scores reflect your understanding of the structure used in your case?

You may be asked to complete and turn in this form to your instructor.

Exercise 14

Athletics and Physical Interdependence Technologies[12]

I. Objective:

To explore differences in interdependence, coordination, and management between various athletic teams.

II. Process:

Step 1. Complete Chart

When the instructor indicates, complete the following chart comparing Baseball, Football, Basketball, and Soccer teams.

	Baseball	Football	Basketball	Soccer
Interdependence (Pooled, Sequential, or Reciprocal)				
Physical Dispersion of Players (High, Medium, or Low)				
Coordination (Type of coordination)				
Key Management Job (Primary focus of management)				

Step 2. Discussion

When directed by your instructor, form groups to discuss the results.

Exercise Feedback Form

Chapter 5   **Exercise #14**

Name: _____   **Student ID:** _____

1. What similarities/differences exist among the four sports in the exercise?

2. What issues arise as a result of the level of interdependence in a department? How might the structure be impacted?

3. How might you assess other team sports (i.e., ice hockey, rugby, etc.) using this approach? Are there other sports that closely resemble those in the exercise in terms of interdependence?

You may be asked to complete and turn in this form to your instructor.

Exercise 15

The Hollow Square

I. Objectives:

To demonstrate problems in the relationship between those who design or create a plan and those who have the responsibility for executing it, to explore the implications of clear communication in a problem-solving task, and to become aware of the factors that promote and inhibit effective problem solving.

II. Process:

Step 1. Group Formation

The class will be divided into one or more teams consisting of planners, operators, and observers. The triads of planner-operator-observer will be identified so people will know with whom they are working.

Step 2. Briefings

Report to the areas assigned by the instructor and read the appropriate briefing sheet for your group. The briefings are found at the end of the exercise.

Step 3. Planning and Instructing

The planners should proceed according to their instructions for the exact length of time stated by the instructor. The operators should work separately, according to their briefing sheet, until contacted by the planners. The observers should meet briefly to divide their responsibilities for observation; they will then take notes on the behavior of the planners and operators. Before the end of Step 3 the planners must call in their operators. The planners will spend at least 5 minutes briefing the operators.

Step 4. Assembly

The operators, working as teams and competing against one another, must assemble the hollow square puzzle as quickly as possible. The team with the fastest assembly time will be declared the winner.

Step 5. Discussion

Planners: Select three adjectives to describe your feelings about the operators.

Operators: Select three adjectives to describe your feelings about planning before the planners called you in, and three for after they called you in.

Observers: Report your perceptions of the operators and planners before they interacted with each other.

Each operating team: Report on the instructions that you received from planners. How did this ultimately affect your ability to assemble the hollow square?

Briefing for Planning Team

Overview

Each of you will be given a packet containing several cardboard pieces that, when properly assembled, will make a hollow square design. During the assigned time you are to do the following:

1. Plan how the 17 pieces distributed among you should be assembled to make the design.
2. Instruct your operating team on how to implement your plan. You may begin instructing your operating team at any time during the planning period—but no later than 5 minutes before they are to begin the assembling process.

General Rules

1. You must keep all of the pieces you have in front of you at all times.
2. You may not touch the pieces held by other team members or trade pieces with other members of your team during the Planning and Instructing Phase.
3. You may not show the "Hollow Square Key" to the operating team at any time.
4. You may not assemble the entire square at any time (this is to be left to your operating team).
5. You are not to mark on any of the pieces.
6. Members of your operating team must also observe the previous rules until the signal is given to begin assembling.
7. When time is called for your operating team to begin assembling the pieces, you may give no further instructions, but are to observe the operation.

Briefing for Operating Team

1. You will have responsibility for carrying out a task for four to six people, according to instructions given by your planning team. Your planning team may call you in to give you instructions at any time. If they do not summon you, you are to report to them when indicated by the instructor. You will be told when to begin your task; after that, no further instructions from your planning team can be given. You are to finish the assigned task as rapidly as possible.
2. While you are waiting for a call from your planning team, it is suggested that you discuss and make notes on the following:
   a. The feelings and concerns that you experience while waiting for instructions for the unknown task.
   b. Your suggestions on how a person might prepare to receive instructions.
3. Your notes recorded on the above will be helpful during the work group discussions following the completion of your task.

Briefing for Observation Team

Overview

You will be observing a situation in which a planning team decides how to solve a problem and gives instructions to an operating team for implementation. The problem consists of assembling 17 pieces of cardboard into the form of a hollow square. The planning team is supplied with the general layout of the pieces. The planning team is not to assemble the parts itself, but is to instruct the operating team on how to assemble the parts in a minimum amount of time. You will be silent observers throughout the process.

Some Suggestions for Observing

1. Each member of the observing team should watch the general pattern of communication but give special attention to one member of the planning team (during the planning phase) and one member of the operating team (during the assembly phase).

2. During the planning phase, watch for such behavior as:
    a. The evenness or unevenness of participation among planning team members.
    b. Behavior that blocks or facilitates understanding.
    c. How the planning team divides its time between planning and instructing (how early does it invite the operating team to come in?).
    d. How well it plans its procedure for giving instructions to the operating team.

3. During the instructing phase (when the planning team is instructing the operating team), watch for such things as:
    a. Who in the planning team gives the instructions (and how was this decided)?
    b. How is the operating team oriented to the task?
    c. What assumptions made by the planning team are not communicated to the operating team?
    d. How full and clear were the instructions?
    e. How free did the operating team feel to ask questions of the planners?

4. During the assembly phase (when the operating team is working alone), watch for such things as:
    a. Evidence that instructions were understood or misunderstood.
    b. Nonverbal reactions of planning team members as they watch their plans being implemented or distorted.

EXERCISE 15   *The Hollow Square*   79

Exercise Feedback Form

Chapter 5   **Exercise #15**

Name: _____   **Student ID:** _____

1. What are some critical elements that a team of planners should consider when it is designing a task for others to carry out?

2. What can the operators do to help the work of the planners, and to ensure that the task is completed accurately and rapidly?

3. In what departments, areas, or divisions of organizations are these problems most likely to occur? Why?

You may be asked to complete and turn in this form to your instructor.

Chapter 6

Exercise 16

Discovering an Organization's Life Cycle

I. Objectives:

To acquire experience in obtaining organizational information from electronic or traditional documentary sources, to become familiar with the organizational development of an actual firm, and to develop an understanding of four stages in the life cycle of organizations.

II. Process:

Step 1. Company Selection

This exercise may be accomplished individually or in groups but, either way, the initial step is to select a business firm. Among the possible sources of firms for this exercise are the various lists of companies maintained by Fortune, Inc., such as the Fortune 500, the Fortune 1000, the Fortune 100 Fastest Growing Firms, and the Fortune Global 500. Your instructor may provide you with an alternate list or a specific company.

Step 2. Research

As directed by your instructor, obtain detailed current and historical information about your assigned firm. Sources of such information are found in library collections of company annual reports, various directories of firms including the series maintained by Dun and Bradstreet, Inc., and the World Wide Web. One possible starting place on the World Wide Web is the Hoover's Online link, which can be found on Fortune's home page (http://www.fortune.com).

Step 3. Analysis

Study the four categories shown on p. 83 and, within the time allotted by your instructor, determine (1) the current life cycle stage of your assigned firm by documenting as many of the characteristics listed on p. 83 as time will permit and (2) the approximate time periods when your assigned firm was at the other stages. In most cases, the classification of a firm will not be uniform. For example, a company may be at the elaboration level in terms of structure and top management style but still at the formalization stage in terms of the other characteristics. Thus, the best strategy is to strive to determine, *in general*, which stage the company seems to be operating in and the time periods of other stages.

Step 4. Report

Describe, for the rest of the class, your assigned firm and your conclusions in terms of the current life cycle of the company and approximate time periods when the company was at other stages.

*Characteristics of Four Life Cycle Stages**

Characteristics of Four Life Cycle Stages	Entrepreneurial	Collectivity	Formalization	Elaboration
General description	Infancy; new and small; energy is devoted to survival	Youth; rapid growth; excited commitment to the firm's mission	Midlife; internal stability and market expansion; delegation with formal systems	Maturity; complete organization with teams; focus on firm's status
Major crisis of the stage	Need for leadership	Need for delegation	Too much red tape	Need for revitalization
Extent of bureaucracy	Nonbureaucratic	Prebureaucratic	Bureaucratic	Very bureaucratic
Structure	Informal; one-person show	Informal with a few procedures	Formal procedures; division of labor; new specialties	Teamwork within bureaucracy; small-company thinking
Products or services	Single product or service	Major product or service, with variations	Complete line of products or services	Multiple product or service lines
Reward/ control systems	Personal/ paternalistic	Personal/ contribution to success	Impersonal/ formalized systems	Extensive/ tailored to product and department
Innovation	By owner-manager	By employees and managers	By separate innovation group	By R&D department
Goal	Survival	Growth	Stability and expansion	Reputation and completeness
Top management style	Individualistic and entrepreneurial	Charismatic and direction-giving	Delegation with controls	Teamwork and attack bureaucracy

* Adapted from Daft, R.L. (2001) *Essentials of Organization Theory and Design*, Cincinnati, OH: South-Western/ Thomson Learning, pp. 101–104 and Exhibit 6.3.

Exercise Feedback Form

Chapter 6   **Exercise #16**

Name: _____   **Student ID:** _____

1. What was the name of the firm that you studied for this exercise? What sources of information did you use to document life cycle stages of this firm?

2. What difficulties did you encounter in collecting information for this exercise and performing the analysis?

3. What are the approximate time periods of the four stages of your firm?

You may be asked to complete and turn in this form to your instructor.

Exercise 17

How Big Are the Colleges?

I. Objective:

To examine the various definitions of organizational size.

II. Process:

Step 1: Compare Colleges

Review the comparison chart (p. 88) of various college characteristics.

Step 2: Rank Colleges

Based upon the statistics provided on p. 88, rank the four colleges in terms of size beginning with the "biggest" college ranked as number one.

Step 3: Group Ranking

Compare your ranks with those of other class members. Attempt to reconcile differences and arrive at a group consensus.

Comparison of Characteristics of Four Colleges

	College A	College B	College C	College D	"Your College"
Total enrollment	33,327	13,715	43,382	10,634	
Undergraduate enrollment	26,075	8,628	31,633	7,994	
Land area	463 a	260 a	2,000 a	1,250 a	
Funded endowments	$286 M	$465 M	$681 M	$3,100 M	
Total faculty	1,897	1,122	1,809	1,057	
Full-time faculty	1,017	774	1,745	726	
Part-time faculty	880	348	54	331	
Total freshmen	5,153	1,859	3,705	1,971	
Acceptance percentage	54%	53%	62%	34%	
Freshman National Merit Scholars	39	12	166	45	
Library volumes	2,310,597	2,000,000	3,401,279	2,704,394	
Library periodicals	15,228	19,551	25,213	24,334	
Library materials expenditures	$5.2 M	$1.8 M	$8.7 M	$6.8 M	
Computers	233	2,000	604	880	
Housing spaces	4,815	3,793	6,779	6,242	
Ranking					

Exercise Feedback Form

Chapter 6   **Exercise #17**

Name: _____   **Student ID:** _____

1. What ranks did you assign to the four colleges?

2. What criteria did you use to assign ranks to the colleges? Why?

3. Develop a composite index of weighted criteria using at least five of the statistics presented. How do the colleges rank when this index is used?

You may be asked to complete and turn in this form to your instructor.

Effective Organizational Control Mechanisms?[13]

I. Objective:

To explore the various considerations of implementing an effective organizational control mechanism and to identify specific criteria that can be used to evaluate the appropriateness of control mechanisms.

II. Process:

Step 1. The Control Mechanism

Your instructor has decided to add to your educational experience by inviting a local business leader to address your class. Aware that your university has a strict parking policy that includes rigorous enforcement of violators ($25 fine), your instructor has decided to request a waiver of the daily parking fee ($1) for this important guest.

Upon further examination, your instructor discovers that the university has developed a control procedure to preclude abuse of the parking fee waiver that includes the completion of a "Request for Complimentary Parking Permits" form.

Step 2. Parking Fee Waiver Form

Review the form and answer the following question: **"What's wrong with this control mechanism?"**

Request for Complimentary Parking Permits

Please provide the information requested below and forward. If you wish to provide a list of persons attending please attach. If you have any questions, contact J. Smith, ext. 1111.

REQUESTING DEPARTMENT: _____

PERSON REQUESTING: _____

PHONE: _____

EVENT: _____

DATE(S): _____

TIME(S): _____

NUMBER OF PERSONS FOR EVENT: _____

PERMITS MAILED OR ISSUED AT INFORMATION BOOTH: _____

JUSTIFICATION FOR WAIVED FEES: _____

_____

_____

APPROVAL/DISAPPROVAL SIGNATURES

Dean: _____   Date: _____

Approve: _____   Disapprove: _____

Vice President: _____   Date: _____

Approve: _____   Disapprove: _____

Exercise Feedback Form

Chapter 6   **Exercise #18**

Name: _____   **Student ID:** _____

1. Is the control cost-effective?

2. Is the control acceptable? Appropriate?

3. Is the process strategic? Reliable and objective?

You may be asked to complete and turn in this form to your instructor.

Chapter 7

Culture and Ethics

Exercise Feedback Form

Chapter 7   **Exercise #19**

Name: _____   **Student ID:** _____

1. Does a company have the right to be interested in employees' off-work behavior? At what point does personal life spill over into work life?

2. Would the type of job make a difference in your recommendation (i.e., an international assignment)?

3. Would you or would you not recommend Morgan? Why?

You may be asked to complete and turn in this form to your instructor.

Exercise 20

Culture in the Land of Doone[15]

I. Objectives:

To enhance participants' understanding of the interpersonal and organizational effects of culture shock and to learn about unfamiliar cultures and why training techniques must fit trainees' cultures.

II. Process:

Step 1. Introduction

Critter Technologies was founded by Ima Critter, a genetic engineer and an entrepreneur. He believes that there is a significant market for Critters. The company uses genetic engineering technologies to manufacture Critters. The purpose they serve is a trade secret. A group of inventors recently created an improved Critter called Critter B, and they hope to sell it to Critter Technologies. The inventors believe that the best way to demonstrate its superiority is to train the company's executives to assemble the prototype. For this purpose, Mr. Critter invited them to visit his facilities in Doone, a unique community located in a remote area of the United States.

Step 2. Preparation

Inventors: Study the prototype of Critter B, determine how you will train the executives to assemble it, and prepare to do so. The executives must be able to assemble the prototype to understand why it is superior to existing Critters. As such, this is the goal of the program.

Executives and observers: Study the information provided by the instructor.

Step 3. Orientation

One inventor visits Doone (the room in which the executives and observers are preparing). He or she meets the executives, describes the upcoming training program, and answers their questions. After visiting for a brief time, the inventor returns to his or her group to finalize preparations.

Step 4. Training

Inventors return to Doone (the room in which the executives and observers prepared), exchange greetings with the executives, and train them to assemble the prototype of Critter B.

Step 5. Discussion

Observers discuss the pertinent elements of the program. Inventors and executives share your observations and explain any noteworthy comments or behaviors, including why you (inventors) selected the particular training methods you used.

101

Exercise Feedback Form

Chapter 7   **Exercise #20**

Name: _____ **Student ID:** _____

1. How does culture shock "feel"? Is it similar to other emotions that people experience? Have you had similar experiences?

2. Describe methods that firms can use to prepare employees for culture shock.

3. What specific elements of organizational culture are especially relevant to situations like the one presented in the exercise?

You may be asked to complete and turn in this form to your instructor.

Exercise 21

A Culture in the Forest[16]

I. Objective:

To become familiar with the basic components of organizational culture by considering an unusual "nonprofit" organizational setting.

II. Process:

Step 1. Introduction

When assigned by the instructor, read the following case of an organization that is widely known although not exactly well documented!

THE ENTREPRENEUR

Robin Hood awoke just as the sun was creeping over the crest of the hill in the very middle of Sherwood Forest. He was not the least rested, for he had not slept well that night. He could not get to sleep because of all the problems he was going to have to face today.

Certainly his campaign against the sheriff was going well, perhaps too well. It had all started out as a personal quarrel between the two of them, but now it was much more than just that. There was a price on his head of 1000 pounds, and there was no doubt that he was causing the sheriff a great deal of trouble, as taxes went uncollected or undelivered to the Crown, and rich men could not sleep soundly at night anywhere near Sherwood.

Things had changed since the early days, however. In those days it was just a small band of men, united in their cause against the sheriff, and for that matter, against Prince John, for the sheriff was simply doing John's bidding. But that was no longer the case. The fame of the Merry Men had grown and with it their numbers. He used to know each man as both a friend and companion, but now he didn't even know all of their names. Little John continued to keep discipline among the men as well as maintaining their skills with the bow, while Will Scarlet kept an eye on the sheriff, as well as any rich prospect who was foolish enough to travel Sherwood. Scarlock took care of the loot as he always had, and Much the Miller's Son continued to keep the men fed.

All this success was leading to problems. Game was, frankly, getting scarce as the number of men in the band increased, and the corresponding demand for food grew. Likely targets for the Merry Men were getting hard to find as more and more wealthy travelers were giving Sherwood a wide berth, as they were reluctant to part with their gold. Finally, the Sheriff and his men were getting better. Robin had always had the advantage of knowing Sherwood better than any man alive, but now there were at least several men who knew it almost as well as he, and some of them wore the colors of Prince John.

All this was leading Robin to reconsider his old ways. Perhaps a simple transit tax through Sherwood might be a part of the answer. But that might destroy his support among the people of the forest, and it had been rejected by the Merry Men, who were proud of their motto "Rob from the rich and give to the poor!" Besides, he needed the support of the poor, as they were his main source of information on the movements of the sheriff.

Killing the sheriff was not the answer. He would just be replaced, and aside from quenching Robin's personal thirst for revenge, the new sheriff might be even more treacherous. Robin hated his enemy, but he had the advantage of knowing the sheriff's strengths and weaknesses. He would not know a new man's talents.

Prince John, on the other hand was vicious tyrant, a good part of which stemmed from his very weakness. The Barons were growing more restless every day, and the people simply hated him. They wanted King Richard back from his jail in Austria. Robin had been discreetly approached by several nobles loyal to Richard to join in the effort to free the King with the promise of a full pardon for him and all his men should they succeed. But Robin knew that if they failed, John would burn Sherwood and the rest of England to the ground to reap his vengeance. Theft and unrest in the provinces were one thing, intrigue at court was another.

Robin knew the days of the Merry Men were numbered. Even as they grew stronger, they grew weaker. Time was on the side of the sheriff, who could draw on all the power of the Crown if he had to, and, if Robin became too much of a threat, would surely do so.

Just then the horn blew for the traditional English breakfast of bread and ale. Robin would have breakfast with the Merry Men and then confer with Will Scarlet, Little John, and Scarlock.

Step 2. Discussion

Discuss the following questions in small groups, or consider them individually, and be prepared to discuss your answers with the class.

1. What are the central values of this culture and what rituals, would you imagine, help to reinforce these values?
2. Who is the hero of the culture of this organization and what networks would be able to support the hero's status?
3. How strong is this culture? Is the culture a dominant feature of the organization as reported? Is the culture "lived by top management"?
4. It would seem as if organizational size has become a major factor in the problems considered by Hood. How has organizational size affected the nature of this organization's culture?
5. Given the issues that Hood is pondering, do you envision any changes in the Band's culture in the near future? Why or why not? If changes are envisioned, what might they be?

Exercise Feedback Form

Chapter 7   **Exercise #21**

Name: _____   **Student ID:** _____

1. What are some of the situations in the environment that will have an impact on whatever Robin decides to do?

2. What are some of the alternatives that Robin is considering for dealing with his problems? Can you identify some additional alternatives?

3. What do you think Robin should do?

You may be asked to complete and turn in this form to your instructor.

Chapter 8

Exercise 22

Dynamics of Change[17]

I. Objective:

To demonstrate the various forms of resistance to change that may occur in an organizational setting.

II. Process:

Step 1. Introduction

Your instructor will provide additional information for you to respond to, both individually and in small groups.

Step 2. Classification

Classify the resultant responses to the instructor provided information using the following list:

1. **Excessive focus on costs.** The mind-set that costs are all-important and that other elements, such as changes to increase employee motivation or customer satisfaction, are unimportant.
2. **Failure to perceive benefits.** Any significant change will produce both positive and negative reactions. If the organization's reward system discourages risk-taking, a change process may falter because employees think that the risk of making the change is too high.
3. **Lack of coordination and cooperation.** Organizational fragmentation and conflict often result from the lack of coordination for change implementation. Moreover, in the case of new technology, the old and new systems may not be compatible.
4. **Uncertainty avoidance.** At the individual level, many employees fear the uncertainty associated with change and will attempt to ignore the change.
5. **Fear of loss.** Managers and employees may fear the loss of power and status or even their jobs.

Step 3. Discussion

Discuss the implications of varied degrees of resistance to change for the organization in small groups. Address specific techniques that may be useful in reducing the impact of resistance to change.

Exercise Feedback Form

Chapter 8   **Exercise #22**

Name: _____   **Student ID:** _____

1. How did you feel after the instructor revealed the purpose of the exercise? Why? Which one of the five barriers to change did you personally experience most strongly?

2. Which one of the five barriers do you believe would be most prominent in a small, entrepreneurial software development company where most employees perform non-routine tasks using specialized skills? Why?

3. Which one of the five barriers do you believe would be most prominent in a large, bureaucratic, labor-intensive manufacturing company where most employees perform routine tasks using non-specialized skills? Why?

You may be asked to complete and turn in this form to your instructor.

Exercise 23

Needle in the Organizational Haystack[18]

I. Objectives:

To learn about the differences between Top-Down (TD) and Bottom-Up (BU) processes for designing and implementing organizational changes and the types of situations for which TD and BU are best suited.

II. Process:

Step 1. Title and Group Assignment

Become acquainted with the exercise and position titles, and receive your title and group assignment from the instructor. Note that reference is made to "top" and "bottom" but that the distinction is relative. The following is an example chain of command that reflects this relativity:

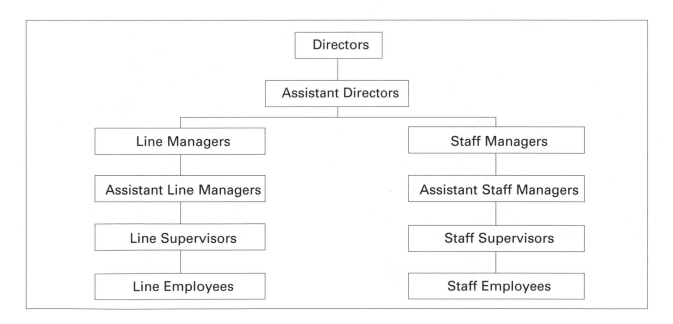

Step 2. Initial Workgroup Meeting

Meet with the members of your workgroup, discuss the rules that pertain to your type of group (TD or BU), and fill out name tags according to the workgroup rules. Workgroup rules are found in the following table.

Type of Rule	TD (Top-Down) Rules	BU (Bottom-Up) Rules
Personal Identity	1. Name tags should have titles only. When titles are identical, alpha names characters should differentiate them (A., B., etc.). Personal names should NOT appear on the tags.	1. Name tags should have first or nicknames with titles in parentheses. Identical titles should not be differentiated.
	2. Place your name tag on the back of your right shoulder if you are a supervisor; otherwise place the nametag on the back of your left shoulder.	2. Place name tags on the front of the right shoulder.
	3. In conversation, use titles only.	3. In conversation, use real names (or nicknames) only.
Communication Patterns	1. Orders (written or oral) are handed down from the top through the chain of command level by level; no unsolicited feedback is allowed; information may be solicited from the bottom by the top but it must be passed through the chain of command.	1. Orders may not be given; rather, information is sought and provided through everyday reciprocal conversation style communication.
	2. Communication may go up only after submitting a request up the chain of command and receiving an approval.	2. Communication may go up and down the chain of command freely, skipping levels if desired.
	3. No voting of any kind; directors make decisions.	3. Decision making by consensus or, if needed, by majority voting.
	4. Persons with identical titles (ignoring any alpha designations) may converse with reciprocal feedback.	4. Persons with identical titles (ignoring any alpha designations) may converse with reciprocal feedback.

Step 3. Locate the Needle

Once the instructor has provided your group with its needle-finding objective, your group should implement its assigned (TD or BU) rules *immediately* without further discussion and begin to achieve the objective by searching the assigned area ("haystack") for the needle.

Step 4. Receive Further Instructions

When your group has either used up all of the allotted time or achieved the objective, return to the instructor's location for further assignments or instructions.

Exercise Feedback Form

Chapter 8   **Exercise #23**

Name: _____   **Student ID:** _____

1. To which type of group were you assigned (TD or BU)? What were the biggest stumbling blocks for your group?

2. What made it possible for your group to make progress toward achieving its objective?

3. Did your group seem to be more organic than mechanistic in operations? Why or why not?

You may be asked to complete and turn in this form to your instructor.

Exercise 24

Environment, Power, and Change[19]

I. Objectives:

To describe the exchanges influencing power differentials in organizations, to understand the four environmental change drivers, and to analyze how change drivers impact ideas and needs and the adoption of change.

II. Process:

Step 1. Review Organizational Change Drivers

The overall theoretical perspective of this exercise is that certain "drivers" directly affect (1) *ideas* and (2) *needs* of organizations as well as the success of (3) *adoption* of changes by increasing organizational member power. These drivers are shown in the following table.

Environmental Change Drivers

Type of Driver	Source of Change Drivers
Social	Issues such as gender, race, age, diversity, or work-family conflict
Political	Pressures to manage public appearance and legal considerations
Economic	Financial pressures on a firm
Technological	Innovations and technological improvements necessary to compete

Step 2. Golf Cart Inc., Five Scenarios

Your organization manufactures golf carts and sells them to country clubs, golf courses, and consumers. Your group is faced with the task of assessing how environmental changes will affect individuals' organizational power. As assigned by your instructor, read each scenario and then identify the five members in the organization (see box on following page) whose power will increase most in light of the environmental condition(s).

1. New computer-aided manufacturing technologies are being introduced in the workplace during the upcoming 2 to 18 months.
2. New federal emission standards are being legislated by the government.

3. Sales are way down; the industry appears to be shrinking!
4. The company is planning to go international in the next 12 to 18 months.
5. The Equal Employment Opportunity Commission is applying pressure to balance the male-female population in the organization's upper hierarchy by threatening to publicize the predominance of men in upper management.

Fifteen Jobs in the Scenario Organizations

Advertising expert (male)	Accountant-CPA (male)	Product designer (male)
Chief financial officer (female)	General manager (male)	In-house counsel (male)
Securities analyst (male)	Marketing manager (female)	Public relations expert (male)
Operations manager (female)	Computer designer (female)	HR manager (female)
Corporate trainer (male)	Industrial engineer (male)	Chemist (male)

Step 3. Group Conclusions

As assigned by your instructor, meet with other members of your group and make a final determination of the five persons whose power would increase most in each of the scenarios.

Exercise Feedback Form

Chapter 8   **Exercise #24**

Name: _____   **Student ID:** _____

1. For each scenario, describe which change driver seems to be affecting the organization.

2. Which organization members did your group select for each scenario? Why?

3. In what way would the selected persons have had an influence on ideas, needs, and the rate of adoption of change in the scenario organizations?

You may be asked to complete and turn in this form to your instructor.

Chapter 9

Decision Making

Exercise 25

Maximizing or Satisficing: Pick the Best—Or the First Good One[20]

I. Objective:

To explore alternative decision-making approaches.

II. Process:

Step 1. Computer Purchase

When told to do so, read the following situational description and place yourself in the role of Connie Heerman, a staff assistant to Betty Ewing, president of Ewing Manufacturing, which is a rapidly growing, medium-sized manufacturer of commercial air-conditioning equipment.

SITUATIONAL DESCRIPTION—PART A

Ewing Manufacturing has decided to discontinue its practice of contracting out its computer and data processing work. Betty Ewing, the president, has decided to purchase a computer system. As staff assistant to the president, you have been charged with evaluating the various systems and making a recommendation as to what computer should be purchased. Ewing's computer needs are very specialized. Regular equipment will not work. The regular computer manufacturers produce these special computers infrequently and the demand is very high. It is a seller's market.

You have contacted eight computer manufacturers and given all of them identical specifications. You find out that these manufacturers will call you when a machine becomes available. Each will quote you a price for a unit that will precisely meet your needs, but these quotes will come in one at a time. You have made some estimates and believe that $500,000, plus or minus $20,000, will be the cost.

Several suppliers will have informed you that they *may* call you within the next three weeks with a price. You will be given a one-time price and you will have 48 hours to accept or reject the offer. If you reject the offer, the computer manufacturer will sell the equipment to another customer. If you accept it, you will receive no other offers. If you reject an offer, you may get some additional ones, but you do *not* know how many quotes you will receive! Since you must have this equipment you will have to take the last offer regardless of price, if you did not agree earlier to purchase one of the units.

You will now start receiving the bids. After each bid is made, place the name of the company and the price in the appropriate column. Then decide whether you accept the offer. Write your acceptance or rejection in the column on the right. Remember the proposals come several days apart and when you turn it down (with the exception of the last one), it will be rescinded.

	Company	Offer	Accept or Reject
1.			
2.			
3.			
4.			
5.			
6.			
7.			
8.			

Step 2. Printer Purchase

SITUATIONAL DESCRIPTION—PART B

Now that you have the computer, you become aware of several new applications for Ewing Manufacturing. With the addition of an online, high-speed printer, you estimate you can significantly improve productivity.

There are several units that seem to meet your needs, according to your research. Most of them have the capability to produce at the level you want. However, there are some differences with respect to durability and maintenance. When you ask the manufacturers for bids, you receive them from only three of the firms.

They are identical bids from each manufacturer. There are some differences between machines with respect to the cost and frequency of repair. The printers from which you can choose follow, with a brief rating of their maintenance records:

Acme Printer — This unit has acceptable performance capability. It has a rating of .25, which is the probability that it will experience a major breakdown within the next three years.

Brilliant Writer — This unit is equally adequate. Its maintenance rating is .20, the probability of a major breakdown within three years.

Clear Writer — This has the same performance capacity as the Acme and the Brilliant—the three-year maintenance rating is .10. Of all machines it is the most dependable.

1. What other information do you need to make a good choice?

_____

_____

_____

_____

Basic Cost of Printer:

Acme Printer   _____
Brilliant Writer   _____
Clear Writer   _____

Compute expected cost of breakdown

Printer	*Breakdown Cost*		*Probability of Breakdown*		*Expected Cost of Breakdown*
Acme Printer	_____	×	_____	=	_____
Brilliant Writer	_____	×	_____	=	_____
Clear Writer	_____	×	_____	=	_____

Total cost computation (transfer the appropriate figures above to the table below)

Printer	*Basic Cost*		*Expected Breakdown Cost*		*Total Cost*
Acme Printer	_____	+	_____	=	_____
Brilliant Writer	_____	+	_____	=	_____
Clear Writer	_____	+	_____	=	_____

Which one is best? _____

2. Are there any circumstances under which you might purchase the Clear Writer, regardless of cost?   ❑ Yes   ❑ No

If so, what are they? _____

Exercise Feedback Form

Chapter 9   **Exercise #25**

Name: _____   **Student ID:** _____

1. If you selected the first computer offered, what reasons can you give for doing so?

2. Did the people who selected the last computer offered make an irrational decision?

3. Do organizations always make rational decisions? Satisficing decisions? Discuss.

You may be asked to complete and turn in this form to your instructor.

Exercise 26

Decisive Decision Making[21]

I. Objective:

To understand ethical frameworks and different perspectives, and to recognize the value of frameworks in decision making while raising awareness of one's own ethical agendas.

II. Process:

Step 1. Read the Exercise

You are the chief seismologist at one of the leading research facilities in North America. You hold a Ph.D. from the most prestigious university in the country specializing in this field. For a number of years, you have been working on perfecting a method for predicting major earthquakes on the West Coast. You report to the director of the research center. The organization is dependent on government agency funds in the form of research grants along with funding from corporate interests.

Recently, you have developed a sophisticated technique that you believe is able to forecast, within 80%, the likelihood of the occurrence of an earthquake during a 48-hour period. The results of a rigorous study that you have just completed indicate that a 7.3-magnitude quake will hit one of four fault lines in Southern California within the next 2 days. Three of the faults are in less populated areas where major damage will be relatively low. However, the fourth fault is the San Andreas, which, if affected, would result in significant damage to structures and a considerable amount of casualties. What is your ethical responsibility regarding the sharing of this information?

Step 2. Rank Order Choices

The following is a list of five alternative strategies. Indicate the action you would take by selecting the most appropriate item, and then rank order the remaining choices. That is, record your first choice by writing the number next to the item, followed by your second choice, and continuing until you have ranked all five options.

_____   Without discussing your findings, hypothetically ask colleagues in your field what they would do in a similar situation. Seek the advice of experts like yourself to confirm your decision; avoid actions that are not supported by your peers.

_____   You must share the information with the media. After informing the research director, it is your responsibility to make sure the news of this potential disaster is released to the public. Notifying the director and other government officials is not sufficient; important information may be withheld. You must be sure the truth is known.

_____   Refer to the procedures and policies manual published by the research institution. If the organization has a policy regarding the responsibility for the disclosure of information, you should follow these procedures.

_____   You must be very careful about the dissemination of your research findings. There is a 20% probability that the quake will not occur, and even if the quake does occur, sharing information could be harmful. You will likely be held responsible for the chaos and panic that may result. Your career is at stake; you cannot afford to be wrong.

_____   You need to calculate the expected costs associated with the quake. That is, you must compare the value of sharing the information openly to that of maintaining silence. Given the probability of the occurrence of the quake, assign estimated values for injuries sustained, resources needed for cleanup, buildings/structures destroyed, and loss of life. Compare these calculations to estimated value related to releasing information. The amount should include an assessment of the reduction of injuries and deaths but should be offset by the costs of preparation and the pandemonium that is likely to result if prior information is known. (Assume you have a computer program that contains the financial estimates; you need only to enter probability.) If releasing information to the public has a higher expected value than remaining silent, then you must divulge your data.

Step 3. Group Discussion

Form groups of four to five students each. Discuss the issues and reach a group consensus, if possible. That is, try to find agreement regarding the rank order of the five choices.

Step 4. Class Discussion

Interact with other groups regarding choices. Discussion should focus on explaining reasons for selections.

Exercise Feedback Form

Chapter 9   **Exercise #26**

Name: _____   **Student ID:** _____

1. What was your first decision choice? Why?

2. Was your first choice consistent with the choices of your group members?

3. Was an observable pattern of choice present in the class? What factor(s) might account for this outcome?

You may be asked to complete and turn in this form to your instructor.

Winter Survival Exercise[22]

I. Objectives:

To compare the effectiveness of several different methods of making decisions and to assess the advantages of group-aided decision processes.

II. Process:

Step 1. Individual Completion

Read the situation and complete the decision form quietly and individually.

Step 2. Form Groups

Form groups of approximately eight members—six participants and two observers. Each group will be assigned a number for purposes of identification.

Step 3. Consensus Guidelines

Your group is to employ the method of group consensus in reaching its decision. This means that the ranking for each of the twelve survival items **must** be agreed upon by each group member before it becomes a part of the group decision. Consensus is difficult to reach. Therefore, not every ranking will meet with everyone's complete approval. Try, as a group, to make each ranking one with which all group members can at least partially agree. Here are some guidelines to use in reaching consensus:

1. Avoid arguing *blindly* for your own opinions. Present your position as clearly and logically as possible, but listen to other members' reactions and consider them carefully before you press your point.

2. Avoid changing your mind just to reach agreement and avoid conflict. Support only solutions with which you are able to agree to at least some degree. Yield only to positions that have objective and logically sound foundations.

Step 4. Group Ranking

Decide upon a group ranking of the items on the decision form. Make a copy of the group ranking with your group designation clearly written on the top.

Step 5. Scoring

Score the individual decision forms in the following way:

1. Score the net (absolute) difference between the participant's answer and the correct answer. For example, if the participant's answer was 9 and the correct answer is 12, the net difference is 3. Disregard all plus or minus signs; find only the net difference for each item.

2. Total these scores; the result is the participant's score. The lower the score the more accurate the ranking.
3. To arrive at an average member score, total all members' scores for each group and divide by the number of members.
4. Put the scores in order from best to worst for each group. This ranking will be used to compare how many members, if any, had more accurate scores than the group's score.

Step 6. Group Ranking

The groups complete their ranking with the group number or name clearly marked on the paper.

Step 7. Correct Ranking

Correct ranking provided.

Step 8. Class Discussion

Share the conclusions of each group in a general session.

WINTER SURVIVAL EXERCISE: THE SITUATION

Your university soccer team has just crash-landed in the woods of northern Minnesota and southern Manitoba. It is 11:32 A.M. in mid-January. The light plane in which you were traveling crashed on a lake. The pilot and copilot were killed. Shortly after the crash the plane sank completely into the lake with the pilot's and copilot's bodies inside. None of you are seriously injured and you are all dry.

The crash came suddenly, before the pilot had time to radio for help or inform anyone of your position. Since your pilot was trying to avoid a storm, you know the plane was considerably off course. The pilot announced shortly before the crash that you were twenty miles northwest of a small town that is the nearest known habitation. You are in a wilderness area made up of thick woods broken by many lakes and streams.

The snow depth varies from above the ankles in windswept areas to knee-deep where it has drifted. The last weather report indicated that the temperature would reach minus twenty-five degrees Fahrenheit in the daytime and minus forty at night. There is plenty of dead wood and twigs in the immediate area. You are dressed in winter clothing appropriate for city wear—suits, pantsuits, street shoes, and overcoats. While escaping from the plane several members of your group salvaged twelve items.

Your task is to rank these items according to their importance to your survival, starting with *1* for the most important item and ending with *12* for the least important one.

You may assume that the number of passengers is the same as the number of persons in your group, and that the group has agreed to stick together.

Winter Survival Decision Form

Rank the following items according to their importance to your survival, starting with *1* for the most important one and proceeding to *12* for the least important one.

_____	Ball of steel wool
_____	Newspapers (one per person)
_____	Compass
_____	Hand ax
_____	Cigarette lighter (without fluid)
_____	Loaded .45-caliber pistol
_____	Sectional air map made of plastic
_____	Twenty-by-twenty-foot piece of heavy-duty canvas
_____	Extra shirt and pants for each survivor
_____	Can of shortening
_____	Quart of 100-proof whiskey
_____	Family-size chocolate bar (one per person)

Winter Survival: Group Summary Sheet

Item	Members						Summary
	1	2	3	4	5	6	
Ball of steel wool							
Newspapers							
Compass							
Hand ax							
Cigarette lighter							
.45-caliber pistol							
Sectional air map							
Canvas							
Shirt and pants							
Shortening							
Whiskey							
Chocolate bars							

Exercise Feedback Form

Chapter 9   **Exercise #27**

Name: _____   **Student ID:** _____

1. Was there anyone who had valuable information who could not persuade others to his or her point of view? If so, why?

2. What factors caused the group to use its resources well—or not well? Who behaved in what ways to influence group functioning?

3. Was there anyone who forced his or her opinion on the group? If so, why was he or she able to do this?

You may be asked to complete and turn in this form to your instructor.

Chapter 10

Conflict, Power, and Politics

Exercise 28

Political Processes in Organizations[23]

I. Objectives:

To analyze and predict when political behavior is used in organizational decision making and to compare participants' ratings of politically based decisions with ratings of practicing managers.

II. Process:

Step 1. Overview

Politics is the use of influence to make decisions and obtain preferred outcomes in organizations. Surveys of managers show that political behavior is a fact of life in virtually all organizations. In this exercise, you are asked to evaluate the extent to which politics will play a part in 11 types of decisions that are made in organizations.

Step 2. Individual Ranking

Rank the 11 organizational decisions listed on the scoring sheet according to the extent you think politics plays a part. The most political decision would be ranked *1*, the least political decision would be ranked *11*. Enter your ranking on the first column of the scoring sheet.

Step 3. Team Ranking

Your instructor will divide the class into groups. As a group, rank the 11 items according to your group's consensus on the amount of politics used in each decision. Use good group decision-making techniques to arrive at a consensus. Listen to each person's ideas and rationale fully before reaching a decision. Do not vote. Discuss items until agreement is reached. Base your decisions on the underlying logic provided by group members rather than on personal preference. After your team has reached a consensus, record the team rankings in the second column on the scoring sheet.

Step 4. Correct Ranking

After all groups have finished ranking the 11 decisions, your instructor will read the correct ranking based on a survey of managers. This survey indicates the frequency with which politics played a part in each type of decision. As the instructor reads each item's ranking, enter it in the "correct ranking" column on the scoring sheet.

Step 5. Individual Score

Your individual score is computed by taking the difference between your individual ranking and the correct ranking for each item. Be sure to use the *absolute* difference between your ranking and the correct ranking for each item (ignore pluses and minuses). Enter the difference in column 4 labeled "Individual Score." Add the numbers in column 4; this score indicates how accurate you were in assessing the extent to which politics plays a part in organizational decisions.

Step 6. Team Score

Compute the difference between your group's ranking and the correct ranking. Again, use the absolute difference for each item. Enter the difference in column 5 labeled "Team Score." Add the numbers in column 5; this total is your team score.

Step 7. Compare Teams and Class Discussion

When all individual and team scores have been calculated, the instructor may record the data from each group for class discussion.

Scoring Sheet

Decisions	1. Individual Ranking	2. Team Ranking	3. Correct Ranking	4. Individual Score	5. Team Score
1. Management promotions and transfers					
2. Entry-level hiring					
3. Amount of pay					
4. Annual budgets					
5. Allocation of facilities, equipment, offices					
6. Delegation of authority among managers					
7. Interdepartmental coordination					
8. Specification of personnel policies					
9. Penalties for disciplinary infractions					
10. Performance appraisals					
11. Grievances and complaints					

Exercise Feedback Form

Chapter 10   **Exercise #28**

Name: _____   **Student ID:** _____

1. Why did some individuals and groups solve the ranking more accurately than others?

2. If the 11 decisions were ranked according to the importance of rational decision processes, how would that ranking compare to the one you completed in the exercise?

3. Is there any evidence from this exercise that would explain why more politics would appear at higher rather than lower levels in organizations?

You may be asked to complete and turn in this form to your instructor.

How You Act in Conflicts

The following items can be thought of as descriptions of some of the different strategies for resolving conflicts. Read each of the items carefully. Using the following scale, indicate how typical each item is of your actions in a conflict.

5 = Strongly Agree   4 = Agree   3 = Neutral   2 = Disagree   1 = Strongly Disagree

_____ 1. I try to investigate an issue with my supervisor to find a solution acceptable to us.

_____ 2. I generally try to satisfy the needs of my supervisor.

_____ 3. I attempt to avoid being "put on the spot" and try to keep my conflict with my supervisor to myself.

_____ 4. I try to integrate my ideas with those of my supervisor to come up with a decision jointly.

_____ 5. I try to work with my supervisor to find solutions to a problem that satisfy our expectations.

_____ 6. I usually avoid open discussion of my differences with my supervisor.

_____ 7. I try to find a middle course to resolve an impasse.

_____ 8. I use my influence to get my ides accepted.

_____ 9. I use my authority to make a decision in my favor.

_____ 10. I usually accommodate the wishes of my supervisor.

_____ 11. I give in to the wishes of my supervisor.

_____ 12. I exchange accurate information with my supervisor to solve a problem together.

_____ 13. I usually allow concessions to my supervisor.

_____ 14. I usually propose a middle ground for breaking deadlocks.

_____ 15. I negotiate with my supervisor so that a compromise can be reached.

_____ 16. I try to stay away from disagreement with my supervisor.

_____ 17. I avoid an encounter with my supervisor.

_____ 18. I use my expertise to make a decision in my favor.

_____ 19. I often go along with the suggestions of my supervisor.

_____ 20. I use "give and take" so that a compromise can be made.

_____ 21. I am generally firm in pursuing my side of the issue.

_____ 22. I try to bring all our concerns out in the open so that the issues can be resolved in the best possible way.

_____ 23. I collaborate with my supervisor to come up with decisions acceptable to us.

_____ 24. I try to satisfy the expectations of my supervisor.

_____ 25. I sometimes use my power to win a competitive situation.

_____ 26. I try to keep my disagreement with my supervisor to myself in order to avoid hard feelings.

_____ 27. I try to avoid unpleasant exchanges with my supervisor.

_____ 28. I try to work with my supervisor for a proper understanding of a problem.

Scoring Table

Type I	Type II	Type III	Type IV	Type V
1.	2.	8.	3.	7.
4.	10.	9.	6.	14.
5.	11.	18.	16.	15.
12.	13.	21.	17.	20.
22.	19.	25.	26.	
23.	24.		27.	
28.				
Total	Total	Total	Total	Total
÷ 7	÷ 6	÷ 5	÷ 6	÷ 4
Avg.	Avg.	Avg.	Avg.	Avg.

Exercise Feedback Form

Chapter 10   **Exercise #29**

Name: _____   **Student ID:** _____

1. Does the conflict style identified by the exercise reflect the approach you take in conflict situations? Why or why not?

2. Did you have two scores that were high? The same? What conclusions do you make about the combinations of styles?

3. How would the style(s) you identified influence your behavior in a conflict with a co-worker? A friend? A family member?

You may be asked to complete and turn in this form to your instructor.

Exercise 30

Prisoners' Dilemma: An Intergroup Competition[25]

I. Objectives:

To explore trust between group members and effects of betrayal of trust, to demonstrate effects of interpersonal competition, and to dramatize the merit of a collaborative posture in intragroup and intergroup relations.

II. Process:

Step 1. Form Teams

Two teams are formed and named Red and Blue. The teams are seated apart from each other. They are not to communicate with the other team in any way, verbally or nonverbally, except when told to do so by the facilitator.

Step 2. Review Tally Sheet (See the form at the end of process steps.)

Become familiar with the payoff schedule and scorecard.

Step 3. Round 1

Round 1 is begun. Teams have three minutes to make a team decision. Do not write your decisions until the instructor signals that time is up.

Step 4. Scoring

The choices of the two teams are announced for Round 1. The scoring for that round is agreed upon and is entered on the scorecards.

Step 5. Rounds 2 and 3

Rounds 2 and 3 are conducted in the same way as Round 1.

Step 6. Round 4

Round 4 is a special round, for which the payoff points are doubled. After representatives have conferred for three minutes, they return to their teams. Teams then have three minutes, as before, in which to make their decisions. When recording their scores, be sure that points indicated by the payoff schedule are doubled for this round only.

Step 7. Rounds 5–8

Rounds 5 through 8 are conducted in the same manner as the first three rounds.

Step 8. Round 9

Round 9 is announced as a special round, in which the payoff points are "squared" (multiplied by themselves: e.g., a score of 4 would be $4^2 = 16$). A minus sign should be retained: e.g., $(-3)^2 = -9$. Team representatives meet for three minutes; then, the teams meet for three minutes. At the instructor's signal, the teams write their choices; then the two choices are announced.

Step 9. Round 10

Round 10 is handled exactly as Round 9. Payoff points are squared.

Step 10. Concluding the Exercise

The entire group meets to process the experience. The point total for each team is announced, and the sum of the two team totals is calculated and compared to the maximum positive or negative outcomes (+126 or −126 points).

Prisoners' Dilemma Tally Sheet

For ten successive rounds, the Red team will choose either an A or a B and the Blue Team will choose either an X or a Y. The score each team receives in a round is determined by the pattern made by the choices of both teams, according to the following schedule.

1. THE PAYOFF SCHEDULE

AX—Both teams win 3 points.
AY—Red Team loses 6 points; Blue Team wins 6 points.
BX—Red Team wins 6 points; Blue Team loses 6 points.
BY—Both teams lose 3 points.

2. THE SCORECARD

Round	Minutes	Choice		Cumulative Points	
		Red Team	Blue Team	Red Team	Blue Team
1	3				
2	3				
3	3				
4*	3 (reps.) 3 (teams)				
5	3				
6	3				
7	3				
8	3				
9**	3 (reps.) 3 (teams)				
10**	3 (reps.) 3 (teams)				

*   Payoff points are doubled for this round.

** Payoff points are squared for this round; retain any minus signs.

Exercise Feedback Form

Chapter 10   **Exercise #30**

Name: _____ **Student ID:** _____

1. Did you worry about being betrayed in this exercise? If so, how did this make you feel?

2. What have you learned about trust in interpersonal, competitive relationships from this exercise?

3. Can you imagine situations where collaboration might not be the most useful approach? If so, what are these?

You may be asked to complete and turn in this form to your instructor.

Endnotes

Chapter 1—Overview of Organization Theory

1. "Associations Exercise: Facilitating Student Participation and Awareness of What They Know in the First Class," Craig C. Lundberg, (1985–86), *The Organizational Behavior Teaching Review, 10,* (1), 92–93.
2. "International Exchange Game: A Hidden Social Dilemma," Don M. McDonald, (2001), *Journal of Management Education, 25,* (4), 425–429.

Chapter 2—Strategy, Design, and Effectiveness

3. "The Manager and the Man: A Cross-Cultural Study of Personal Values," G. W. England and N. C. Agarwal, (1974), Kent, OH: Kent State University Press, 29–32.
4. "Organizational Diagnosis: Fast Food Technology," R. J. Lewicki, D. D. Bowen, D. T. Hall, and F. S. Hall, (1988), *Experience in Management and Organizational Behavior,* New York: John Wiley and Sons, Inc., 224–227.
5. "Examining Social Responsibility: A Trade-Off Among Stakeholders," Joe G. Thomas, (1992), *Journal of Management Education, 16,* (2), 250–253.

Chapter 3—Organization Structure

6. "Organizing Exercise #12," H. L. Tosi and J. W. Young, (1982), *Management: Experiences and Demonstrations,* Homewood, IL: Richard D. Irwin, Inc., 75–79.
7. "Creative Sentence Corporation," R. L. Daft and K. M. Dahlen, (1984), *Organization Theory: Cases and Applications,* St. Paul, MN: West Publishing Company, 76–79.
8. "Organization Structure and Design: The Club Ed Exercise," Cheryl Harvey and Kim Morouney, (1998), *Journal of Management Education, 22,* (3), 425–429.

Chapter 4—Environment

9. "Instrument: ID Scales," M. Saskin and W. C. Morris, (1984), *Organization Behavior,* Reston, VA: Reston Publishing Company, Inc., 234–238.
10. "Environmental Influences," R. R. McGrath, (1985), *Exercises in Management Fundamentals,* Reston, VA: Reston Publishing Company, Inc., 187–190.

Chapter 5—Technology

11. "Measures of Perrow's Work Unit Technology: An Empirical Assessment and a New Scale," M. Withey, R. L. Daft, and W. H. Cooper, (1983), *Academy of Management Journal, 26,* (1), 45–63.
12. "Relationships Among Interdependence and Other Characteristics of Team Play," (Exhibit 6-12), R. L. Daft (2001), *Organization Theory and Design,* Mason, OH: South-Western/Thomson Learning, 222.

Chapter 6—Size, Life Cycle, and Control

13. "An Out-of-Control Organizational Control Mechanism," H. Eugene Baker III and Kenneth M. Jennings, (1994), *Journal of Management Education, 18*, (3), 380–384.

Chapter 7—Culture and Ethics

14. "My Friend Morgan: An Exercise in Ethics," Nancy E. Landrum, (2001), *Journal of Management Education, 25*, (3), 606–616.
15. "Training in the Land of Doone: An Exercise in Understanding Cultural Differences," David S. Hames, (1998), *Journal of Management Education, 22*, (3), 430–436.
16. "Case 1: Robin Hood," (1999), *Annual Editions: Management 99/00*, Guilford, CT: Dushkin/McGraw-Hill, 43.

Chapter 8—Innovation and Change

17. "Dynamics of Change: Precipitated Resistance to Change in the Classroom," H. Eugene Baker III, (1988–89) *The Organizational Behavior Teaching Review, 13*, (4), 134–137.
18. "A Class Exercise Highlighting Thompson's Three Types of Interdependencies," Alan L. Brumagim, (1995), *Journal of Management Education, 19*, (4), 508–512.
19. "Power and the Changing Environment," John E. Barbuto, Jr., (2000), *Journal of Management Education, 24*, (2), 288–296.

Chapter 9—Decision Making

20. "Decision Making Exercise #26," H. L. Tosi and J. W. Young, (1982), *Management: Experiences and Demonstrations*, Homewood, IL: Richard D. Irwin, Inc., 159–164.
21. "Decisive Decision Making: An Exercise Using Ethical Frameworks," Mark Mallinger, (1997), *Journal of Management Education, 21*, (3), 411–417.
22. "Winter Survival Exercise," D. W. Johnson and F. P. Johnson, (1982), *Joining Together: Group Theory & Group Skills*, Englewood Cliffs, NJ: Prentice-Hall, Inc., 111–118.

Chapter 10—Conflict, Power, and Politics

23. "Political Processes in Organizations," R. L. Daft and M. P. Sharfman, (1990), *Organization Theory: Cases and Applications*, St. Paul, MN: West Publishing Company, 339–341.
24. "Confirmatory Factor Analysis of the Styles of Handling Interpersonal Conflict: First-Order Factor Model and Its Invariance Across Groups," M. A. Rahim and N. R. Mace, (1995), *Journal of Applied Psychology, 80*, (1), 122–132.
25. "Prisoner's Dilemma: An Intergroup Competition," J. W. Pfeiffer and J. E. Jones (Eds.), (1974), *A Handbook of Structured Experiences for Human Relations Training*, San Diego, CA: Pfeiffer and Company, 52–56.